THE
BIG
BOOK
OF
BIBLE TRUTHS 2

THE
BIG
BOOK
OF
BIBLE TRUTHS 2

SINCLAIR B. FERGUSON

CF4·K

The Big Book of Stories and Bible Truths
God Jesus and You
ISBN: 978-1-84550-372-7
© 2008 Sinclair B Ferguson
Published in 2008 by Christian Focus Publications, Geanies House, Fearn, Tain,
Ross-shire, IV20 1TW,
Great Britain.
www.christianfocus.com
Cover design by: Daniel van Straaten
Printed by: Bell and Bain
Illustrations by: Fred Apps

Remembering

IAN MACDOUGALL

who enjoyed these stories,
recorded them,
and
made this book possible.

Contents

A BIBLE ARCHITECT

What Do Architects Do?

Do you know what architects do? They design buildings. There is a wonderful church building in the centre of the city of Glasgow. It was designed by a man called Stark. It is called 'St George's Tron'. If you came out the back door there were green fields. But now it's in the middle of a large city. All you can see are large buildings, shops, restaurants, traffic and lots of people.

Now, St. George's Tron isn't very big. There are other buildings that are far bigger. Is it very tall? No – skyscrapers in New York are much, much taller. However, the architect who designed the church made it a special size. Can you guess what size he made it? Let me give you a clue.

King Solomon

In the Bible we read about another architect, King Solomon. He built the Temple in Jerusalem. This was a special building for God. God's people went there to worship him. God would come to the Temple to meet with them.

When Solomon built the Temple people didn't measure things in metres or yards. They used a measurement called a cubit. When Solomon built his temple it was sixty cubits long by twenty cubits wide. A cubit was about eighteen inches or forty-five centimetres.

Now, St. George's Tron church in Glasgow is about the same size as Solomon's temple. Isn't that amazing! Did Mr. Stark want to remind this congregation that they belonged to the same church as the Old Testament believers?

READ: 1 Corinthians 3: 16

LESSON: God's temple is not a building made of stones. God's temple is made out of people who love and worship him.

The apostle Paul tells us in 1 Corinthians 3: 16 that there is something even more amazing than these buildings.

Paul said, 'God is now building a much better temple that is going to spread all over the world. You are God's temple.''

Peter says, 'God isn't using ordinary stones any longer – he's using living stones – men and women, boys and girls and he's fitting them all together.'

When we all fit together in the church family, we become God's temple. God comes and meets with us and we praise him and we worship him and we love him. God meets with his people wherever they are. We don't need buildings! God will meet with his people wherever they meet together.

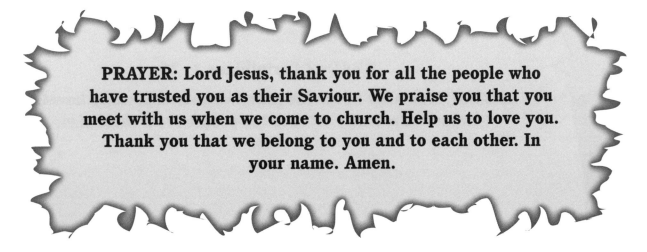

PRAYER: Lord Jesus, thank you for all the people who have trusted you as their Saviour. We praise you that you meet with us when we come to church. Help us to love you. Thank you that we belong to you and to each other. In your name. Amen.

THE BIGGEST PROMISE

We've Done It

Do you know what a 'high five' is? You see it when you watch a basketball game on television or an American sport like baseball. When somebody hits a home run in baseball and the ball goes off the field the player will go back to his team mates in the dugout and they'll put their hands up and go - smack against his! And sometimes they shout, 'Yes!'

When they do this they mean, 'We've done it!'

READ: 2 Corinthians 1: 20

LESSON: How God keeps his promises and especially how God keeps his promise to save his people from their sins.

God's Promise

God has made lots of promises. The Bible is full of them. But how do we know that God is going to keep his promises? We know that he is going to keep them because he kept the biggest promise of all. The biggest promise that our Heavenly Father has made is that he would send his own Son, Jesus, to die on the cross so that our sins would be forgiven.

I'm Thirsty

When Jesus was dying on the cross, right at the end, he asked for a little drink. He was so tired and it was so difficult for him to speak. He said, 'I'm thirsty.' Somebody came and gave him something to drink, so that his mouth wouldn't be dry and so that he could speak. Then, in a very loud voice he said, 'It is finished!' What he meant was 'Yes! I've done it'. He had died for all of our sins on the cross. God's biggest promise, that he would send Jesus to be our Saviour, had been kept.

Because God has kept his biggest promise, we can be absolutely sure that he will say, 'Yes!' to all his other promises too.

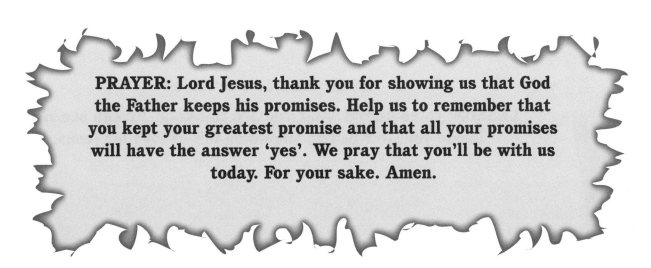

PRAYER: Lord Jesus, thank you for showing us that God the Father keeps his promises. Help us to remember that you kept your greatest promise and that all your promises will have the answer 'yes'. We pray that you'll be with us today. For your sake. Amen.

ABBREVIATIONS

Using a Letter Instead of a Word

Do you know what an abbreviation is? An abbreviation is when you use a letter or a few letters instead of using the whole word. .

AV stands for The Authorised Version of the Bible. This Bible was first printed in 1611 when James the Sixth of Scotland, and the First of England, was king. It was authorised by him to be read in the churches. That is how it came to be known as the 'authorised version'. Christians in other countries call it the 'King James Bible.'

Do you know what CV means? It means *Curriculum Vitae*. The words mean the course of your life - all the things that have happened to you. When you are older and apply for a job you may be asked for a CV – in which you tell what has happened in your life.

DV stands for two other Latin words: *Deo Volente*. These mean 'God willing'. Someone might say, 'We are going do this, DV.' 'We're going to do this, God willing – if God wants it to happen.'

A Plane Journey

One Friday morning I was in the United States and decided to email a friend of mine. I said, 'I will get to Glasgow on Saturday at 8.45 a.m.' I also told him I was flying first into Chicago and then I was flying to Glasgow.

When I was flying into Chicago the wheels of the plane came down. We were about to touch down on the runway. But suddenly the plane went away up in the air

READ: Matthew 6: 25–34

LESSON: Jesus knows what you are thinking. He can see right inside you. Our hearts should be full of love for Jesus.

again! We circled our way round Chicago. Finally the captain came on the intercom and said, 'You'll be wondering what happened.'

Well, we were wondering what happened! He said, 'As I was about to land, I saw there was another plane on the runway just in front of us.'

Help!

I suppose if he had waited another second or two, I might not have got back to Glasgow on Saturday morning. There would have been an accident instead.

This reminded me that my life is not in my hands. It's in God's hands. I thought to myself, 'I don't know what the future holds but I know God holds my future. I must put my life in God's hands.'

It's safe to put our lives into God's hands. Although we don't know exactly what his will is for tomorrow, he knows. And he has promised never, ever, ever to leave us and never to forsake us.

So when you think of abbreviations like AV and CV remember that the best abbreviation of all is DV.

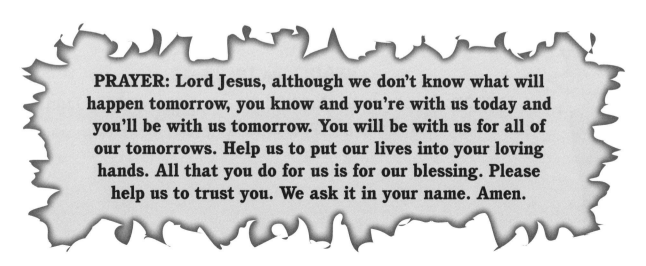

PRAYER: Lord Jesus, although we don't know what will happen tomorrow, you know and you're with us today and you'll be with us tomorrow. You will be with us for all of our tomorrows. Help us to put our lives into your loving hands. All that you do for us is for our blessing. Please help us to trust you. We ask it in your name. Amen.

MOST VALUABLE PERSON

MVP

Do you know what an MVP is? An MVP is a Most Valuable Player or Person. You might award this title to someone who plays best at a football match. But who is the most valuable person to you? The most valuable person in the world is the Lord Jesus. Who is the next most valuable person? Before you guess, here are some clues:

1. This MVP tells you hundreds of these ... Bible Stories.

2. This MVP changes six thousand of these ... Nappies.

3. This MVP makes seven thousand of these ... Dinners.

4. This MVP washes fifteen thousand of these ... Socks.

READ: John 19: 25–27

LESSON: We are to be thankful for our mums and our families. God has given us people to care for us.

12

5. This MVP says even more of these ... Prayers for you.

6. Who do you think this MVP is? Your mum, of course!

Be Thankful

Next to the Lord Jesus there is nobody in the world more important than your mum. She has done all these things - the meals, the socks, lots of things for you. She does it because she loves you! How about giving your mum a great big hug, and saying 'thank you for loving me. I love you too.' Or maybe you can tell your dad or your grandma - whoever it is that cares for you and loves you today.

I am thankful for my mum. I'm thankful for those people who have cared for me in the past and who love and care for me today. I know you are thankful too. Do you ever thank the Lord Jesus for them?

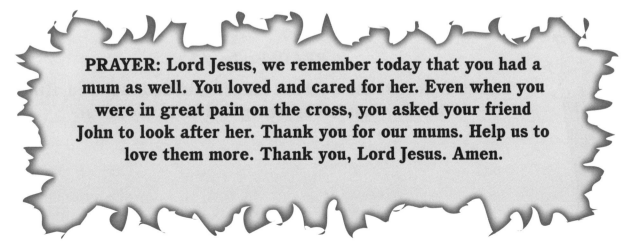

PRAYER: Lord Jesus, we remember today that you had a mum as well. You loved and cared for her. Even when you were in great pain on the cross, you asked your friend John to look after her. Thank you for our mums. Help us to love them more. Thank you, Lord Jesus. Amen.

THROUGH THE SEA

God's Path

Psalm 77, verse 19 is one of the most interesting verses in the Book of Psalms. It tells us something about God. 'Your path led through the sea.'

Do you remember when God's people were taken out of Egypt and across the sea? 'Your path led through the sea though your footprints were not seen.'

Sometimes God works in our lives and leads us in ways that we don't understand. Sometimes we can't even see what he is doing. If I walked on mud you would be

READ: Psalm 77

LESSON: Sometimes we don't understand God. But God always knows what is happening and he is in control.

able to see my footprints. But if you could walk on the sea, you wouldn't leave any footprints! Sometimes we can't understand what God is doing. That's true especially when difficult things or sore things happen to us. When that happens we can still trust God even though we cannot understand what he is doing.

When you say, 'Where are you going, God? I can't see your footprints', he will say to you, 'Trust me, because I know what I am doing. I know where I am leading you. Follow me. One day you will see where my footprints were heading all the time.'

PRAYER: Lord, you know everything about us, our past and our future. Even though we sometimes don't understand you, please help us to trust you. Thank you that you've shown us in Jesus that we can always trust you. Fill us with your joy and forgive our sins. We ask it for Jesus' sake. Amen.

THE BODY

Jesus is the Head

In Ephesians chapter 4, verse 4 Paul says that the church is like a body. How is the church like a body? What do we have on top of our bodies? A head. Now, if the church is a body, who do you think is the head? What happens in the head? The head is where all the orders come from. Who is head of the church? Jesus is the head of the church. So that's one way that the church is like a body. Bodies have got heads and Jesus is the head of the body. He's the one who tells us what to do.

How the Body Works

There's another way the church is like a body. What happens if someone comes up to you with their fist clenched and punches you right in your face? What does your body do? It collapses. What do you do if somebody tries to do that to you? You protect yourself with your hands or with your arms.

If you get hurt in the leg, or if you get kicked, does your hand go down to rub it? That is how a body works – when one part gets hurt, other parts of the body rush to help the part that's hurt.

That's also how the church works. When people in the church get hurt, the other parts of the body of Jesus rush to help and protect the part of the body that has been hurt or damaged.

What happens if you go to a football stadium and your team scores a goal? Does everybody just sit down and fold their arms? No. Their whole bodies stretch

READ: Ephesians 4: 1–6

LESSON: The church is like a body. Jesus is in charge.

upwards and they shout – 'It's a goal!' People get excited and praise the team they support. That's how the body works. When something good happens, the whole body gets excited and says, 'Great!'

We belong to the body of Jesus, the church. When something wonderful happens to someone who belongs to Jesus we say, 'That is absolutely wonderful!'

Because we all belong to the same body, we all have the same head who is Jesus. We care for each other when sad and bad things happen. We get excited for each other when wonderful and good things happen. And that's what it means to belong to the body that is the church.

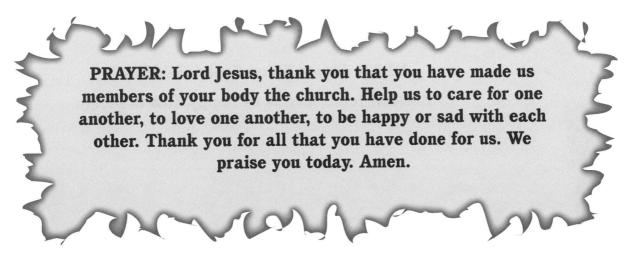

PRAYER: Lord Jesus, thank you that you have made us members of your body the church. Help us to care for one another, to love one another, to be happy or sad with each other. Thank you for all that you have done for us. We praise you today. Amen.

ARE YOU HAPPY?

A Question For You

In chapter 5 of his book, James, the brother of Jesus asks, 'Is anyone happy?'

Well let's ask ourselves that question. Are we happy?

Why do we get happy? What makes us happy?

When good things happen to us like holidays, or birthdays – then we are happy.

Some people gave me a lovely plaque with my name on it. Whenever I look at it I think of the Christian friends in Korea who gave it to me.

I received something else once that made me happy. It was from the boys and girls in our church Sunday school. They drew pictures of themselves and wrote out some Bible verses for me.

So there are lots of things that make us happy but what do we do when we're happy? What is it that makes you feel happy? When something makes you happy, you feel like something is rising up inside you - then you smile. The smile rises up inside you and then it pushes out onto your face! You smile because you're happy. Why do we smile? Why do our faces show when we are happy?

It's because God made us this way. He gives us all the things and the people that make us happy.

When we're happy God wants us to have more than just smiley faces. He wants us to share our happiness with others. And he wants us to share it with him.

James asked another question...'If you are happy, why don't you sing?' Singing is another thing we want to do when we are happy.

READ: James 5 and Zephaniah 3: 17

LESSON: Jesus makes us happy. God is happy.

Singing

When you're happy because the Lord Jesus is with you all the time, you can sing to him and say, 'Lord Jesus, I'm so happy because you are so good and kind to me.'

Here is something to do when you're on your own in your bedroom or out for a walk. Think about all the good things the Lord Jesus has given you and just sing to him.

The Lord Jesus loves that. There's an amazing verse in the Bible that says, God is so happy about having us as his children that he sings about us. (You can read it in Zephaniah 3:17, near the end of the Old Testament).

Are you happy? 'Then,' says James, 'how about some songs?'

PRAYER: Lord Jesus, thank you that you're such a wonderful Saviour and such a wonderful friend. You have given us so many wonderful things to enjoy – our families; friends and our church. We want to sing your praises and thank you for who you are and what you have done. We pray this in your name. Amen.

A DAD AND HIS BOY

A Journey

One day Abraham said to his son, Isaac, 'I am going to take you somewhere special and we are going to have a very special service.' The two of them went off. They got up early in the morning and rode away. They rode all day and they rode all the next day. What do you think Isaac was saying? Probably 'Are we there yet, Dad?'

A Mountain

Finally they got to the foot of a mountain called Mount Moriah and they began to climb it. They had three things with them. Isaac was carrying some wood, because they were going to make a sacrifice to God. Abraham had the fire because they were going to burn the sacrifice. He also had a knife because in the Old Testament they killed the sacrifice.

No person or animal wants to be sacrificed. So Abraham also had ropes. He would use these to tie the sacrifice onto the altar that he was going to build.

When they were half way up the mountain, Isaac looked up at Abraham and said, 'Dad, I have got the wood, you've got the knife and the fire but there is something missing. Where is the sacrifice?'

Abraham had a great secret he hadn't shared with his son. Isaac himself was going to be the sacrifice. 'But he couldn't tell that to Isaac, could he?

Instead Abraham said, 'God will provide a sacrifice for us, Isaac. Let's keep going.'

READ: Genesis 22

LESSON: Abraham didn't need to sacrifice his son. God was willing to sacrifice his son, Jesus. Jesus was willing to die.

A Sacrifice

Isaac kept going because he trusted his father, Abraham. He trusted him so much that when they got to the top of the hill he let his dad tie the ropes all round him. Abraham stretched his son out on the altar. As Isaac looked up he saw that his dad had a knife in his hand. God had said 'Go and sacrifice Isaac.'

Just as he was about to do it, God said 'Stop!' When Abraham turned round there in the bushes was an animal that God had provided. He took Isaac off the altar and put the animal on there instead.

Why should there be such a strange story in our Old Testament? Here is the reason. It is to tell us that Abraham didn't need to sacrifice Isaac. God was willing to sacrifice his only son, Jesus, to save us from our sins.

That mountain was called Moriah. It was the same place where later on the city of Jerusalem was built. That was where Jesus made a sacrifice for our sins. Long before it happened, Abraham and Isaac were given a glimpse of what Jesus and his Father would do for us at Calvary.

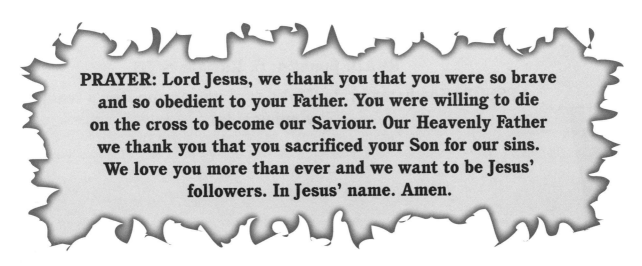

PRAYER: Lord Jesus, we thank you that you were so brave and so obedient to your Father. You were willing to die on the cross to become our Saviour. Our Heavenly Father we thank you that you sacrificed your Son for our sins. We love you more than ever and we want to be Jesus' followers. In Jesus' name. Amen.

WINNING

Scoring Goals

A couple of months ago I was at a special dinner party for all the boys who were with me in school. This year I saw my old friend, David, who also used to live across the road from me. After school we loved to play football together in the street. Those were the good old days when you could play football in the street without getting run down! I had only one problem with David and that was his dad. He had been a really good football player. He often got home from work earlier than all the other dads. If we were playing football on the street he'd join in. If David's dad was playing against your team you had no chance of winning!

READ: James 4: 6; Romans 8: 31

LESSON: God hates pride. Make sure you are on God's team - the winning side.

Who God Plays Against

In the Bible, the book of James says, 'If God opposes you, you've no chance of winning.' Let's think about one of the teams that God is playing against. It's called 'Team Pride'. God doesn't like it when we are proud. He is always on the other side. If you are proud then that's the team that you are on. You are on Team Pride – the losing team!

But there is good news. In Romans 8: 31 Paul tells us, 'If God is for us, who can be against us?' And in James 4: 6 it says 'God who opposes the proud, gives his grace to the humble.' So when we say to God, 'Oh God, there's still pride in my heart. Please help me to think about the Lord Jesus and how he was humble and not proud', then God says, 'I will be with you'.

No matter what happens to you, no matter what the opposition is, if God is for us we are on the winning side! Our problems will be defeated. Isn't that great!

Maybe at school someone will say 'Where were you on Sunday?' Will you tell them that you were at Sunday school? Perhaps they will laugh when you tell them. Remember this, God is for you. You will not be a loser if God is for you!

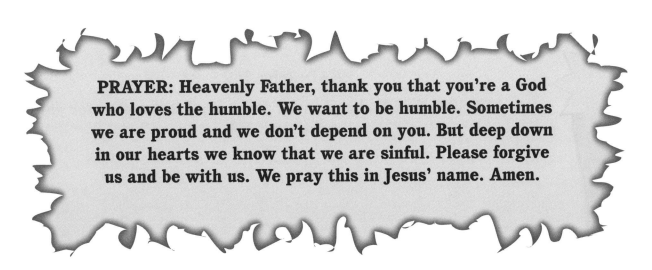

PRAYER: Heavenly Father, thank you that you're a God who loves the humble. We want to be humble. Sometimes we are proud and we don't depend on you. But deep down in our hearts we know that we are sinful. Please forgive us and be with us. We pray this in Jesus' name. Amen.

GOD SAYS IT IS TIME

Jesus' Time

One day some nasty people tried to seize Jesus. Can you imagine that? They hated the Lord Jesus so much that they wanted to get rid off him. They were angry with Jesus, because of what he said and did. They tried to seize him but 'his time' had not come. They couldn't get hold of him. Eventually they would kill him. But on this occasion they couldn't do it. Jesus' 'time' had not yet come.

Do you know what that means?

READ: John 7: 25–31

LESSON: God had a plan for Jesus. God has a plan for you.

24

It doesn't mean that Jesus looked through his bag and got out his clock and said, 'It's not time yet! Jesus knew that there was a different kind of clock from the clocks that we use, and the watches that we have. God has got a clock. And God had on his clock all the things that he wanted Jesus to do, and all the things that would happen to Jesus. God had a plan in his mind of how it would be for Jesus. He had planned when Jesus would come into the world. Then at a certain time Jesus would die for our sins. Until God's time arrived nobody could seize Jesus. God had his hand on everything that happened. As these people were trying to seize Jesus it was as if God said 'I'm not going to let you do that'. God's plan for Jesus was perfect.

God also has a plan for you - a marvellous one. God's plan always works out the way God wants. So when you get upset, or when disappointing things happen you can say, 'My Heavenly Father has a plan, and he's working out his plan for my life day by day. Somehow or other this must be part of God's plan for my life'.

So, as Christians we are able to look up into heaven and say 'Heavenly Father I don't really understand what's going on. But I know that you have a plan for my life. I know this must be a part of your plan. Help me to live for you so that one day I'll look back and say 'God did that. It was hard at the time – but God really knew what he was doing!'

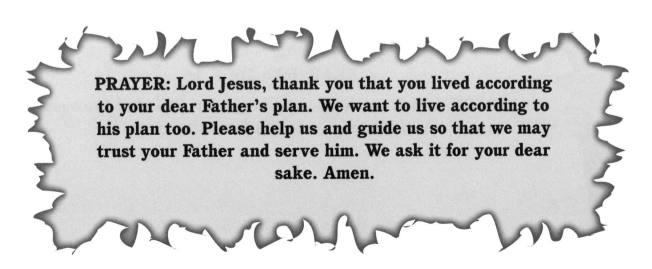

PRAYER: Lord Jesus, thank you that you lived according to your dear Father's plan. We want to live according to his plan too. Please help us and guide us so that we may trust your Father and serve him. We ask it for your dear sake. Amen.

IS GOD EVER BORED?

Too Busy to be Bored

Is God ever bored? How do you know the answer to that question? Do you ever get bored? Does your mum ever get bored? Perhaps your mum would say – 'I am far too busy ever to get bored'. Maybe that's part of the answer to the question, 'Does God ever get bored?' God might say, 'I'm far too busy looking after you to get bored!' God's been looking after the world for a long time. He's still doing it today. So I don't think God ever gets bored.

READ: John 16: 5–16

LESSON: God is too busy to be bored but he is not too busy to listen to you and to look after you.

God's Biggest Secret

Is God ever lonely? He's got to look after the whole universe, including you, all on his own. But God never gets lonely or bored because God is never on his own.

After three years teaching his disciples, Jesus let them into God's biggest secret. He is different from us. He is one God but three different persons: the Father, the Son and the Holy Spirit. Even before he made the world the Father was with his Son and with his Holy Spirit.

Is that hard for you to understand? It's hard for me to understand too! But we can be sure that God never gets bored because he always has company in himself. God the Father, the Son and the Holy Spirit.

Sometimes when you are spending time with friends you forget what time it is. Suddenly one of you will shout out, 'Look at the time! I was supposed to be home an hour ago!' I think it must be like that for God the Father, with his Son and with his Holy Spirit. They enjoy each other so much that they never get bored.

However, there is something even more wonderful than that! The Father and the Son and the Holy Spirit, one God, were talking together before the world was made. They knew we would sin and do wrong things. When they were talking together about this, the Father said to the Son, 'Would you go into the world and die on a cross to save these people?'

The Son said to the Father, 'Father, I'm willing to do that but the Holy Spirit must also be sent into the world so that people will come to trust me and love me. He will give them power in their lives to live for me.'

That's how we get to know God as Father, Son and Holy Spirit. When you know God you'll know that God never gets lonely or bored. But as well as that you'll know that you will never be lonely. And you don't ever need to be bored when he is with you!

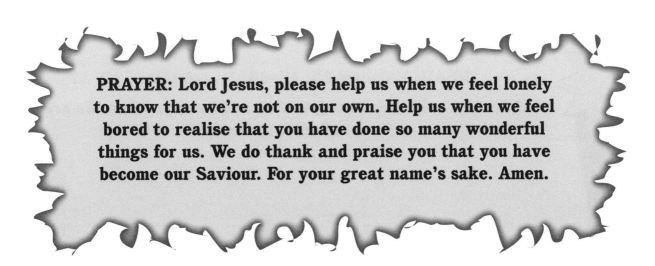

PRAYER: Lord Jesus, please help us when we feel lonely to know that we're not on our own. Help us when we feel bored to realise that you have done so many wonderful things for us. We do thank and praise you that you have become our Saviour. For your great name's sake. Amen.

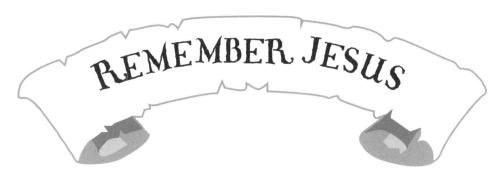

REMEMBER JESUS

One Big Family

When Christians get together from different parts of the world they know that they belong to the same family.

The disciples knew what this felt like. So did Paul.

READ: Matthew 26: 17–30; 1 Corinthians 10: 17

LESSON: Christians belong to God and to each other. We are part of one big family.

28

On the night before Jesus was going to die, he spent time with his disciples. They had a meal together. Jesus took a loaf of bread and shared it among the disciples. He explained to them that his body would be crucified and die for them.

As the bread was passed around each disciple took a little bit from the same loaf. This taught them that just as all the bits of bread belonged to one loaf – so all Christians belong in the one family.

Years later Paul and the other Christians had the same kind of meal. They remembered Jesus and his death. As they celebrated this special meal Paul and the other Christians also took a little bit of bread each and ate it together. They all took it from the same loaf. Paul said, 'Because there is one loaf, we, who are many, are one body, for we all eat of the one loaf.'

Bible Bread

This special meal is something that Christians still eat today. They each take a bit of bread from the same loaf. When they do this they are to remember that each Christian is part of one big group of people. Every Christian belongs to every other Christian. If you belong to Jesus then for the rest of your life you will also belong to all the other people in the Christian family all over the world. That's one of the marvellous and fantastic things about being a Christian.

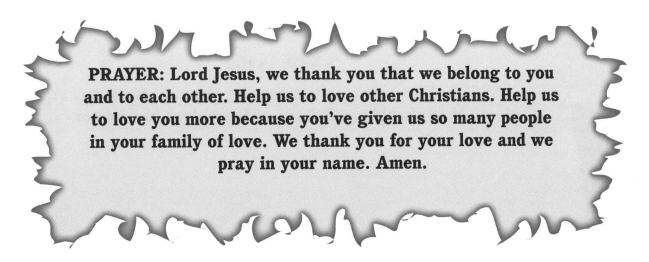

PRAYER: Lord Jesus, we thank you that we belong to you and to each other. Help us to love other Christians. Help us to love you more because you've given us so many people in your family of love. We thank you for your love and we pray in your name. Amen.

THE HEAVENS DECLARE

The Glory of God

The Bible tells us 'The heavens declare the glory of God.' That means it's as though the sky, and the marvellous things that are in the sky, are all praising God.

What do you see when you look at the sky in the daytime? The sun. Then at night what do you see? The moon. And what else do you see? Stars! Together they are like a great orchestra. They are all praising God so far away in the sky.

Not everybody hears the music. Not everybody looks up into the sky at night and sees the stars and says, 'They're singing the praises of our Lord Jesus Christ who put all the stars there.' Or 'Look at that great big ball of fire! It's on fire praising God.' Sadly, some people are like radios that have never been 'plugged in' – so they don't hear this music.

READ: Psalm 19

LESSON: When you look at the sky, the sun, moon and stars, they should remind you of Jesus' love and power.

30

Get Plugged In

So, there's all this wonderful music going on – the stars, and the sun and the moon – they're all praising God. But unless we get 'plugged in' we will not be able to hear. So how do we get 'plugged in'?

We get 'plugged in' when we come to trust in the Lord Jesus who made all these things. He made all that music. When we come and trust in the Lord Jesus, we don't just look up at the sky at night and say, 'Boy, they're far away!' We look up at the sky at night and say, 'Wow! My Saviour Jesus put all these things there so that they could praise him and so that I could look up and know about his power and his love.'

Jesus, God's Son, has made all these wonderful things that we can see through telescopes. He wants us to trust in him because he loves us and cares for us.

Now where do we find out about Jesus? We can only find out about Jesus when we look up at the stars if first of all we find out about Jesus by looking down at our Bibles!

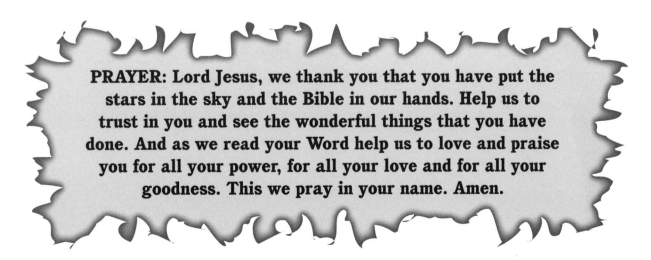

PRAYER: Lord Jesus, we thank you that you have put the stars in the sky and the Bible in our hands. Help us to trust in you and see the wonderful things that you have done. And as we read your Word help us to love and praise you for all your power, for all your love and for all your goodness. This we pray in your name. Amen.

JESUS' MUM IN A TIZZY

What is a Tizzy?

Do you know what a tizzy is? I looked up my dictionary to find out what a tizzy was. To be in a tizzy means to be 'in a nervous state'. Does your mum ever get into a tizzy? Most mums and most dads get into a tizzy. Mums get into a tizzy usually when there are just too many things to do. Does your mum get in a tizzy trying to get you ready for school or church? Nobody likes being late.

READ: John 2: 1–11

LESSON: Do what Jesus tells you.

A Wedding Celebration

One day Jesus' mum, Mary, was with him and some of his friends at a wedding.

Have you ever been at a wedding? Did you enjoy it? Weddings are good unless you're in a tizzy. And Jesus' mum was really in a tizzy.

Unlike our weddings, this wedding celebration had gone on for a whole week. That was normal in Bible times. Because the celebrations had lasted so long all the wine ran out before the party was over! That was why Jesus' mum went into a tizzy.

What did she do? She did the first thing you need to do if you're ever in a tizzy – she asked Jesus to help. And then she said something to the people who were there at the wedding. Here are five letters to help you remember just what Jesus' mum said. D W J T Y. It means DO WHAT JESUS TELLS YOU. And that's exactly what they did.

There were huge water containers in the house. Jesus said, 'Fill those containers up with water'. They must have wondered why they were filling them up with water when everybody wanted wine. But they did what Jesus said. They filled them up. Then Jesus told them to pour some out and take it to the person in charge. When they did the water had turned into wine! The party could go on!

Remember D W J T Y.

Whenever you're in a tizzy Do what Jesus tells you!

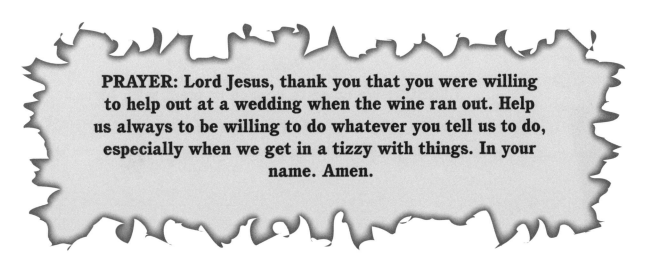

PRAYER: Lord Jesus, thank you that you were willing to help out at a wedding when the wine ran out. Help us always to be willing to do whatever you tell us to do, especially when we get in a tizzy with things. In your name. Amen.

I WILL DECLARE

Why do we Come to Church?

My church isn't the only church where Jesus is a member. But that's why I come. It's nice to see friends, isn't it? But we come not just to see each other; we come to meet with the Lord Jesus.

Why do we come to meet with Jesus? Well, he has promised us that he will be with us. Jesus said, 'I will be there with you all.'

READ: Psalm 22: 22–24

LESSON: We come to church to meet with Jesus.

What do you think Jesus does during the church services? We can't see him but we know he's here. Is he just sitting back thinking, 'The singing's not too good today,'? Or even, 'That was a pretty average sermon?'

Hebrews chapter 2, verse 12 tells us what Jesus does when he meets with his people!

He Will Declare his Name to his Brothers.

How does Jesus speak to us in church? Well, he speaks to us when we talk about what he says in the Bible and when the Bible teachers are talking to us about the Lord Jesus.

Have you ever listened to the preacher or Sunday school teacher but felt that at the same time there is another voice that is speaking right into your heart? That's what Jesus says he's doing. 'I will declare your Name to my brothers.' So when we come to church, Jesus is the person who does the real preaching and the real teaching.

Jesus also says, 'in the congregation I will praise you.' Do you ever share a hymn book with someone in church? You are both looking at the same book so that you can see what words to sing. Now, when we sing together in church it's like singing and sharing our hymn book with Jesus. Jesus is saying, 'Come on, now. You can praise God better than that. I'm hearing you and I'm leading the worship today!'

So whenever you come to a church where Jesus also comes to church, listen for his voice and sing together with the Lord Jesus.

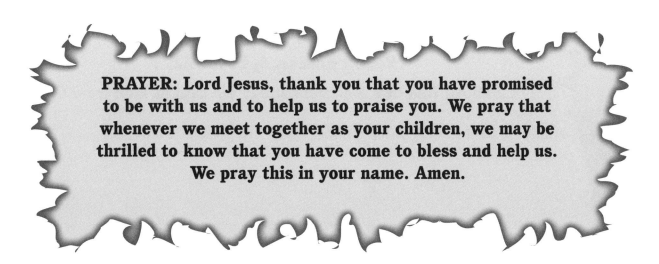

PRAYER: Lord Jesus, thank you that you have promised to be with us and to help us to praise you. We pray that whenever we meet together as your children, we may be thrilled to know that you have come to bless and help us. We pray this in your name. Amen.

ADAM AND EVE HIDE

Hide and Seek

I am sure you have played hide and seek for fun. But do you also hide in real life? Perhaps you don't want to go to school. You pull the duvet over your head and hide! You remember you haven't done your homework and you just want to run away. But you can't, can you?

We want to hide when we are afraid, or when we've done something wrong. You are afraid of what might happen to you if you are discovered. Most of us hide when we've done something wrong and we're afraid of being found out. We hope that if we hide our problems will all go away.

READ: Genesis 3; Psalm 32: 7

LESSON: God can see everything. We cannot hide from God.

Hiding from God

Right at the beginning of the Bible, in Genesis chapter 3, we read about what happened to Adam the first time he did something wrong. Adam and Eve both knew they had disobeyed God. They were frightened and so they hid from God.

Later on that day God came to the Garden of Eden to speak with Adam. But Adam could not be found. God called out, 'Adam! Where are you?' Foolish Adam was trying to hide from the God who had made the whole universe! Where was he hiding? Behind a bush! But the God who had made the whole universe had also made the bush that Adam was hiding behind. Was there any point in Adam trying to hide? No. The God he was trying to hide from could see everything.

God saw Adam and said, 'Adam, what are you doing behind that bush?'

Adam said, 'I did something wrong and I was afraid.' That was why Adam hid.

Hiding in God

But what should we do instead of hiding from God?

Psalm 32: 7 tells us what to do. David had been hiding from God for months because he'd done something very wrong. Finally he realised that he couldn't possibly hide from God. But there was somewhere he could hide. Instead of hiding *from* God, he could hide in God.

Have you ever done something that was wrong and hidden from your dad? Because you knew you couldn't hide from him forever, you thought of running away from home. But instead of running away you ran to your dad and said, 'I'm sorry.'

Did he put his arms around you? Instead of having to hide from your dad anymore, you were hiding in him.

David realised that when you've done something wrong God knows about it. We want to run away and hide because we're afraid that we've let God down. But instead of hiding from him, we should go and hide in him. He will put his arms around us and say, 'I forgive you and I'm going to help you.'

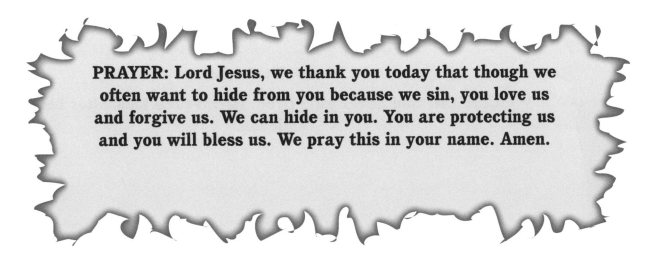

PRAYER: Lord Jesus, we thank you today that though we often want to hide from you because we sin, you love us and forgive us. We can hide in you. You are protecting us and you will bless us. We pray this in your name. Amen.

GOD NEVER SLEEPS

How Much Sleep do you Need?

Have you noticed how little babies seem to spend most of the time sleeping? If you have a little brother or sister maybe sometimes you hear a little cry in the middle of the night. Perhaps you wake up too or maybe you just turn over in bed and think 'Well, mum and dad can look after the baby.'

When babies grow up they still wake people up, but this time they often wake up too early. Their mum and dad yawn and say 'Get back to bed'. However, a few

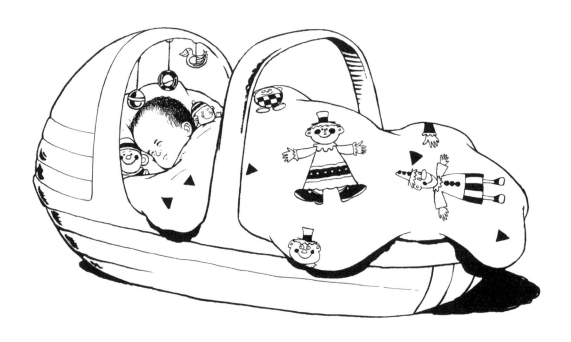

READ: Psalm 121

LESSON: God never gets tired. He loves to look after his children.

years after that something very strange happens. Older children don't want to go to bed – isn't that right? But then in the morning they don't want to get up!

Albert Einstein was a very clever man. He spent a lot of time during the day thinking and working out problems. He was a very clever scientist. After he died they decided to weigh his brain to find out how heavy it was. It was quite a bit heavier than the average brain! But because he spent a lot of time thinking with his brain he also spent a lot of time sleeping. Albert Einstein needed ten hours sleep every night! Once he had spent all that time sleeping he was refreshed and ready to spend lots of time thinking the next day.

How Much Sleep Does God Need?

Now, think about all the things God does. He is looking after our world. He is looking after the stars that we can see in the sky at night and the planets. Then there are all kinds of things we can't see. He is looking after those too. But, God doesn't need any sleep. He never gets tired; he never gets stuck; he never goes in the huff and says 'I am going to bed and am not going to talk to anyone.' Sometimes mums get exhausted looking after just one baby. But God never ever, ever, ever gets exhausted, never gets tired, never gets sleepy. And he just loves to look after his children.

When you put your head down on the pillow to go to sleep, remember he is awake, and he is watching over you . He will never, ever take his eye off you.

Isn't it wonderful to have a God who does not need sleep?

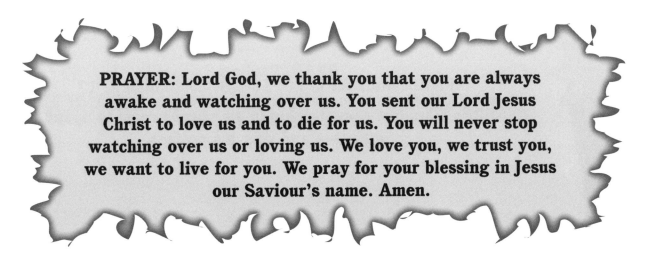

PRAYER: Lord God, we thank you that you are always awake and watching over us. You sent our Lord Jesus Christ to love us and to die for us. You will never stop watching over us or loving us. We love you, we trust you, we want to live for you. We pray for your blessing in Jesus our Saviour's name. Amen.

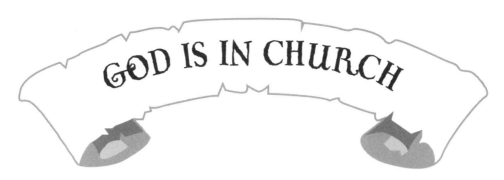

GOD IS IN CHURCH

When God Doesn't Enjoy Church

One day, Jesus went to the church in Capernaum. He was asked to preach that day. While he was preaching there was a man full of an evil spirit who started shouting at him. I wonder if God enjoyed being in that service?

Sometimes God doesn't enjoy being in church. How do I know that? Well you can read about this in the very last book of the Old Testament. This is what God said to the people who were going to church in those days, 'I wish that somebody would come and shut the church doors. Although the people are coming to the building, they're not really coming to be with me which is the really important thing.'

Now, of course, we come to church to be with each other. But most of all we come to be with God. These people were just coming to church on the outside and not coming to God on the inside. So there are some times when God doesn't really like coming to church. He'd rather somebody just shut the doors.

When God Does Enjoy Church

What happened next? Well Malachi tells us that those who really loved the Lord talked about him with each other. The Lord listened and said, 'We need to write down the names of those who are saying nice things about me. They will be mine in the day when I make up my treasure.'

So sometimes in Malachi's day, God didn't like going to church. But sometimes when the people were loving him and praising him and wanting to be with him God loved being there.

READ: Malachi 1: 10; 16–18. Zephaniah 3: 17

LESSON: When we come to church we should come to spend time with God and sing his praises.

The prophet Zephaniah says, 'When the Lord loves coming to church, he takes great delight in you. He rejoices over you with singing.'

Did you know that God likes singing? Do you ever sing to God? Do you ever sing about how wonderful he is? You listen to music and hum along because you like what you hear. Sometimes God is so happy because we're praising him that he sings along with us because he loves to hear us singing.

Can you really believe that God loves you as much as that? Well, if he sent his Son to die for us, we can be absolutely sure that he loves us that much. So when you're singing to God in church or in Sunday school, ask this question, 'Does the Lord like my singing today? Am I really praising him or am I grumpy?' Think about whether your singing is pleasing God - because if it is - God is singing along with you.

PRAYER: Lord Jesus, we thank you that you love us and we pray that as we sing your praises you will love to hear us sing about your goodness, power and faithfulness. So Lord, help us not only to enjoy being together but to enjoy being with you and praising you. We ask this in your name. Amen.

THE EARLY CHURCH

Work It Out

After Judas had betrayed Jesus there were eleven apostles left. But altogether there were about 120 disciples of Jesus in Jerusalem. On the day of Pentecost another 3,000 people became Christians. That's 120 plus 3,000. Then later on we are told how many men were in the church. Not people, men – and that number was 5,000. But the church wasn't just made up of men. There would have been women and children too. So we can see from these numbers that the church was growing. More and more people were trusting in Jesus.

Now, let's imagine that if there were 5,000 men there would have been about 5,000 women and they probably had about two children each. So you multiply 5,000 by 4 which is 20,000.

How Many Churches?

So there were probably 20,000 people in the Jerusalem church. They met in homes. How many people do you think could meet together in a big house? I suppose a really big house with a garden could have about 300 people.

So let's say there were 300 in each church. How many 300s are there in 20,000? You will need to get out your calculator to work out this sum. The number you get will be 66.666. That's sixty-seven churches! The apostles did the preaching and teaching in these sixty-seven churches. At first there were only eleven of them. So each apostle must have had to teach in at least six churches. Many of these churches were meeting every day so perhaps the eleven apostles were teaching every day in all sixty-seven churches. That's a lot of teaching!

READ: Acts 2: 1–13

LESSON: Everybody should do something in church.

Too Much Work

On top of that, they had to organise all these churches. So one day the apostles said, 'We're going to get some other people to do things in our churches.' And that's what they did. They said, 'We can't do everything – we're not the only Christians here. We need to get other people involved.'

So they looked for people who were filled with the Spirit of Jesus and said, 'Let's get these people involved.'

What do you think happened next? They actually ended up with even more churches than before! Why was this? It's simple – other people were now involved.

It's like that in every church. It's wrong to think that the minister should do everything. Everybody in the church should be doing something.

Is there something you can do?

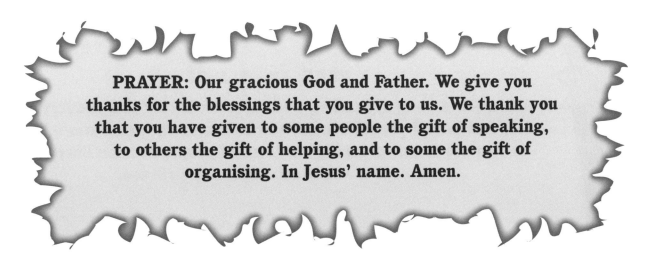

PRAYER: Our gracious God and Father. We give you thanks for the blessings that you give to us. We thank you that you have given to some people the gift of speaking, to others the gift of helping, and to some the gift of organising. In Jesus' name. Amen.

WHAT IS A REVIVAL?

When God Comes in an Amazing Way

A long time ago two boys lived in a town called Coleraine in Northern Ireland. Let's call them Jimmy and Sammy. God was working in this city. One day when the two boys were in their classroom at school, Jimmy was very upset. He wasn't concentrating on his work. Jimmy tried to get on with his work but all of a sudden he just burst into tears.

The teacher – we'll call her Mrs McClutchie – sighed and said to him, 'Come out here, Jimmy.'

Jimmy shuffled up to her big high desk where she quietly asked him, 'Jimmy, what's wrong with you, today?'

This is what Jimmy said, 'Mrs McClutchie, I am so sad because of my sins.'

Well, Mrs McClutchie didn't know what to say. Jimmy was still crying. After a few moments Mrs McClutchie decided that Jimmy should go back home to speak to his mum and dad.

She pointed to Sammy who was still sitting at his desk.'Sammy,' she said, 'close your books, put them on the desk and you take Jimmy home.'

Now, Sammy had been worried about his sins as well. But he had told the Lord Jesus about them. He had said to Jesus, 'Lord Jesus, please forgive my sins and make me clean in my heart and help me to serve you.' So Sammy was already a Christian. He knew just what to say to help Jimmy:

READ: Acts 8: 1–25

LESSON: A revival is when God comes to a city or a country and lots and lots of people become Christians at the same time. When God comes in this amazing way lots of people become Christians, not just adults but boys and girls too.

'Jimmy, if you trust the Lord Jesus and ask him to forgive you, he'll forgive all your sins. We should pray to Jesus about your sins right now.' And that's exactly what they did. They prayed together, 'Lord Jesus, thank you for dying for Jimmy on the cross. He wants to have his sins forgiven and he wants to trust you.'

Jimmy began to trust the Lord Jesus. Can you guess what they did next? They said, 'Let's go back to school.'

Mrs McClutchie was absolutely amazed. She said, 'What's happened?'

'Oh Mrs McClutchie,' Jimmy exclaimed. 'I'm so happy because my sins have all been forgiven!'

Mrs McClutchie wasn't sure what to say to Jimmy so she told him to get on with his work. But just then another boy put his hand up and said, 'Please Miss, may I leave the room?' Then another boy did the same. Then one of the girls, 'Please Miss, may I leave the room?'

Within half an hour almost everybody had left. None of them came back. Mrs McClutchie didn't know what to think. So she stood up on her chair and looked out the window. All the boys and girls in the class were sitting on the ground praying that the Lord Jesus would forgive their sins.

Mrs McClutchie immediately went to get the minister. It didn't take long for the news to spread. Mums and dads and many other people began to turn up at the school. They saw what was happening and soon they were asking the boys and girls, 'How can we get our sins forgiven?' Nobody left the school until 11 o'clock at night. Many of them went home happy that their sins had been forgiven.

Now if somebody in your school were to say to you, 'I'm so unhappy about all the wrong things I've done,' - do you think you'd be able to tell them what Sammy told Jimmy about the Lord Jesus? I hope so.

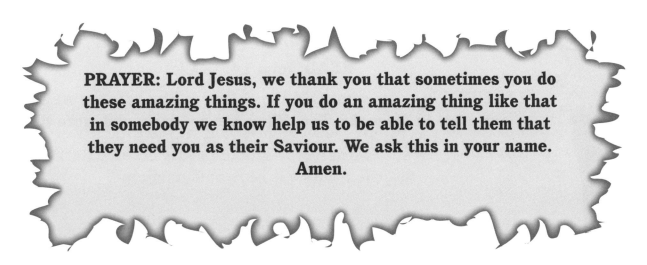

PRAYER: Lord Jesus, we thank you that sometimes you do these amazing things. If you do an amazing thing like that in somebody we know help us to be able to tell them that they need you as their Saviour. We ask this in your name. Amen.

SEE ME SEE THE FATHER

My Friend David

I have a friend whose name is David. He is a small man who wears spectacles. He is very clever and very serious. He always gets straight to the point.

One day I was in a church in the same country that my friend David comes from. I was standing at the front of the church and saw someone walking towards me. He was a small man with round spectacles. When he came and spoke to me he was very serious and he got straight to the point! Do you know what I said to him? 'You must be my friend David's father.'

He said, 'How did you know?'

Well, I couldn't say, 'Because you're small, you wear round spectacles, you're very serious and you get straight to the point,' could I? But that was the truth! Because I knew David, as soon as I saw this man and saw his spectacles, and heard him speak I knew this must be David's father.

This reminded me of what Jesus said, 'If you have seen me, if you know me, if you know what I am like, then you know exactly what my Heavenly Father is like.'

READ: John 14: 9–14

LESSON: We know what God the Father is like because we know and trust in Jesus, his Son. When we get more and more like Jesus others discover what God is like too.

At the Train Station

One day I was waiting at a train station. There was a man standing near me. I could hardly believe it. He looked just like a friend of mine who had died a few years before. His face was the same, his hair was the same – he was jingling coins in his pocket just like my friend used to do, and he was whistling. My friend always whistled. I stood and looked at him and thought to myself, 'He looks exactly like my friend, only a little bit older.'

I wondered, 'Will I or won't I?' 'Will I or won't I?'

Quietly I walked over towards him. Then I was standing right next to him.

'Excuse me,' I said, smiling. 'Are you by any chance, the brother of my friend?'

And he said, 'Yes.'

It was his brother! How did I know it was his brother? Because he was so like his brother, my friend.

The Heavenly Father

We know what our Heavenly Father is like because we know Jesus. Other people also discover what Jesus is like when they see us getting more and more like him. We are in Jesus' family, and we remind people of him!

Wouldn't it be wonderful if your friends began to think about the Lord Jesus because they saw that you are like him?

PRAYER: Lord Jesus, thank you that you've shown us your Heavenly Father and that by your Spirit you are able to make us more like you, our dear elder Brother. We pray that you would do this so that others may know that we belong to your family and will want to belong to it too. And we ask this in your name. Amen.

Crucifixion

When people died by being crucified, it took a long time. One of the things that the Romans did in order to shorten that time was to beat the people they were going to crucify. That meant that they would die more quickly. We know what they did to their prisoners because we read about this in the Gospels. This is what they did to Jesus Christ. We also read about it in other places. The Romans themselves wrote down what they did to their prisoners. In the Gospels and in these other books we can find out exactly what they did to the Lord Jesus Christ before his crucifixion.

READ: John 19: 1–3

LESSON: Jesus was willing to suffer and die so that we could be saved from our sins.

Pontius Pilate gave the orders to have Jesus flogged. His soldiers stripped him and then got him to bend over, and put his back down. They then took a whip which had sharp little stones and pieces of metal in it. A very strong man, or perhaps several men, then started to beat Jesus across the back – again and again and again. That must have been terrible – absolutely terrible.

When you think about that and about what happened to our Lord Jesus, do you ever ask, 'Why did God let that happen? Couldn't God have sent some angels that would have hit the soldiers and saved Jesus?' Well, he could have. Jesus himself said, 'God could send thousands of angels to save me if I asked him to stop this.' So why did God let that happen? Why did Jesus let that happen to him?

The answer to that question is this: Jesus went through all that because he loves you. Isn't it absolutely amazing that the Lord Jesus was prepared to suffer so much, to die in our place, to take away our sins just because he loves us so much?

PRAYER: Lord Jesus, we can hardly bear to think about the terrible things you suffered. We want to thank and praise you that you loved us so much that you were prepared to be our Saviour. May we always love, serve and obey you. We ask this for your sake. Amen.

MASTER CRAFTSMAN

Jesus' Parents

When Jesus came into the world, who were the two people who looked after him? One was, of course his mother, Mary and the other was Joseph.

What did Joseph do for a living? How did he make money to feed his family? He was a carpenter.

READ: John 5: 19–24; John 1: 3

LESSON: Jesus made the whole world and came into that world as a helpless baby.

When Jesus was a little boy, I'm sure he went into Joseph's carpenter's shop to watch him work. John 5: 19 is one of my favourite verses in the Bible. It says that Jesus' relationship, his love for his Heavenly Father, was a little bit like his love for Joseph his stepfather. In those days if your father was a carpenter then you probably became a carpenter. So this is why Jesus says, 'The Son does what he sees his Father doing.'

The Carpenter's Shop

Joseph made things with his hands and he was a master craftsman. If someone had gone into Joseph's carpenter's shop and said, 'Excuse me, I want to meet the master craftsman,' I suppose Joseph would have said, 'That's me. I'm the master craftsman here. My name is above the door. I can make anything you want. I can build you a house of wood. I could make you a rocking horse. I could make you a chair or a table. I could just make you anything out of wood because I am the master craftsman.'

If you had gone into that carpenter's shop and seen Jesus, you would have thought, 'This boy must be the master craftsman's apprentice who is just learning the trade.' But the truth of the matter was that it was Joseph who was the apprentice and Jesus who was the master craftsman ! John 1: 3 says everything in the world was made by Jesus!

That is really hard to understand, isn't it? The one who made everything was sitting beside Joseph's bench watching him make things with wood. Joseph was a master craftsman with wood but he was really just learning how to be Jesus' apprentice. All through his life, the Lord Jesus would show Joseph how to be an apprentice to the Person who had created the whole world.

So will you remember that Jesus is the Person who made the whole world? The little baby who was lying in the manger was the person who made the wood for the manger, and made the whole world.

If he can do that, he can do anything, can't he?

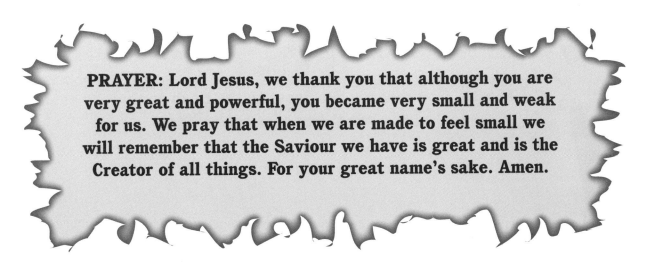

PRAYER: Lord Jesus, we thank you that although you are very great and powerful, you became very small and weak for us. We pray that when we are made to feel small we will remember that the Saviour we have is great and is the Creator of all things. For your great name's sake. Amen.

GOD'S LANGUAGE

What Language do you Speak?

People in the United Kingdom, America, Australia, New Zealand, Canada and other places all speak English. Can you speak other languages too? Some people speak German, Dutch, French, Italian and Spanish. In Scotland there is another language that some people speak. It is called Gaelic.

Now here is another question. Do you think God understands all these languages? Yes, he does! He understands all languages so that whenever anybody prays in one of these different languages, God hears that language and answers prayer.

A Language Without Words

When we speak we use words. But do you know a language where you do not speak any words? Sign language doesn't use spoken words. This is a language that is used by people who cannot hear. When someone is speaking with sign language they use their hands instead of their tongue. All the letters and words have special hand signs.

There is another kind of language we sometimes use – it is the kind of language you use when Mummy and Daddy ask you to do something and you put an angry scowl on your face. It's the kind of language you use if you are trying to do something and it doesn't work. Your face scrunches up and you stamp your feet! It's the kind of language you use when you say goodbye to your mum and dad when you really wish you were going with them. Your face is all crumpled up and your mouth is down at the ends.

What kind of language do we call that? It's called 'body language'. It's a kind of sign language that shows what we really think.

READ: John 1: 1–14

LESSON: God sent his Son Jesus in the flesh so that we could see what God was really like.

a b c d e f g

h i j k l m n

o p q r s t u

v w x y z

If we are happy what kind of body language do we use? We smile. If we are sad what kind of body language do we use? We look sad – or we frown.

God's Language

Did you know that God has used body language? The Lord Jesus is God's body language.

Even if we cannot understand other languages, the most important language to understand is God's body language. God sent his Son to take a human body and to live in a human body. In this way we see what the invisible God is like. Because Jesus was sent by God we can understand what God is really like. God's Son took a human body and died on the cross. So God's body language tells us that he loves us more than anything.

PRAYER: Lord Jesus, we thank you that you have shown us what you are really like. You died for us in your body on the cross in order to forgive our sins and to make us new. You rose again from the dead to be our living Saviour for evermore. Help us to trust you and love you for ever. We ask this for your great name's sake. Amen.

GOD'S PLANS

A Magnificent, Amazing, Time Machine

Imagine that you own a time machine and are travelling back in time on your first adventure. After a few minutes you see Queen Victoria! You must have travelled over 100 years! Suddenly it's the year 1492. You look out the window and see Columbus sailing across the Atlantic. Then it's the year 1314 and outside the battle of Bannockburn is being fought. Everything is going so fast you hardly have time to draw breath.

All of a sudden you see a shining light in the distance! You ask, 'Is that a star? Is that Bethlehem? Hurray! I've reached Bible times!' Then you zoom past Daniel in the lions' den and David with his sheep. You see Moses, Joseph and Abraham for just a few minutes. The time machine finally begins to slow down. You have gone right back to the beginning of the Bible.

Just as Adam and Eve begin to disappear you see a brilliant flash of light and the whole world disappears. There is nothing to be seen… and then you hear a voice.

God the Father is speaking to his Son. Let's listen to what is said:

'After we've made them,' he says, 'they're going to sin.'

'Father, we'll have to rescue them,' is the Son's reply.

The Father says to his Son, 'Yes, let's make a plan.'

'Father,' says the Son, 'We can share the plan.'

I think we can hear the Holy Spirit saying, 'I'll help too.'

God the Father then announces 'Here is the plan…'

On the time machine screen you see a picture of a manger. What does that mean?

READ: John 17: 24; Ephesians 1: 4; 1 Peter 1: 20

LESSON: God had a plan to save sinners right from before the world was even created.

God the Father says, 'Son, you will need to become a little baby and go to the smallest and the poorest. Only when you do this and live a perfect life from the beginning will we be able to rescue the boys and girls and the mums and dads from their sins. Will you do that? Will you become a baby in a manger?'

'Father,' says the Son, 'Of course, I will.'

Another picture appears on the screen. It's a star. Why would God need a star?

'I will send a star because I want wise men to come from the east,' God the Father says. 'They won't have a Bible. They won't know that I have promised to send you. I want people from all over the world to learn about how you will rescue them. Will you go into the world and be the Saviour?'

The Son says, 'Father, of course! I'll go into the world.'

'My Son,' God the Father says, 'there is a third part of the plan. It is a cross.'

Now why would God the Father need a cross?

'This plan needs a cross,' says the Father, 'because only if you are prepared to die on the cross for the sins of the world will it be possible for us to rescue them from their sins. I will bring you back to life again but you must first die on the cross for their sins to save them. Would you do that for them? Would you do that for me?'

The Son says to his Father, 'Of course. I will do it. And the plan will work.'

Of course you don't need a time machine to find out about the plans God made. We read about them in God's Word, the Bible. We read about Jesus and about how the plan God made worked out.

But if you really did have a time machine we'd turn back for home now and we'd be talking together for ages about our amazing adventure!

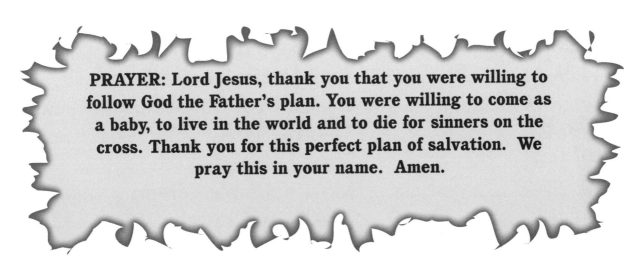

PRAYER: Lord Jesus, thank you that you were willing to follow God the Father's plan. You were willing to come as a baby, to live in the world and to die for sinners on the cross. Thank you for this perfect plan of salvation. We pray this in your name. Amen.

Bible Reading Index
Old Testament

New Testament

* These stories have two Bible readings

OTHER BOOKS BY SINCLAIR B. FERGUSON

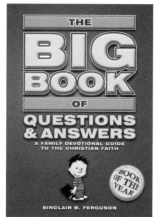

Questions! Questions! Questions! Children are full of them. Where did I come from? What is God like? Is there only one God?

The Big Book of Questions and Answers is a family guide to the Christian faith. It contains a wealth of activities, prayers, and Bible references. This interactive resources material will bring families closer together as they learn about the Christian faith.

Sinclair B Ferguson is Senior Minister of The First Presbyterian Church of Columbia, South Carolina. He is also Distinguished Visiting Professor of Systematic Theology at Westminster Theological Seminary. He was formerly minister of St George's-Tron Church, Glasgow.

ISBN: 978-1-85792-295-0

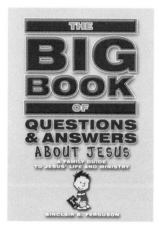

Following on from the success of the original *Big Book of Questions and Answers,* this book tackles the many questions that children have about Jesus, including:

What was special about Jesus?
Why did Jesus heal sick people?
Why did Jesus have to die?
How can I give my life to Jesus?
An answer is given for each question, accompanied by a page of reading and a memory verse. To help the children take the message on board there are activities and suggestions for discussion. Prayers are also given to encourage them to bring every aspect of life to their Heavenly Father.

An invaluable tool for introducing children to Jesus and helping them to get to know Him better, in an enjoyable and interactive way.

Short listed for 'Christian Children's Book of the Year'.

ISBN: 978-1-85792-559-3

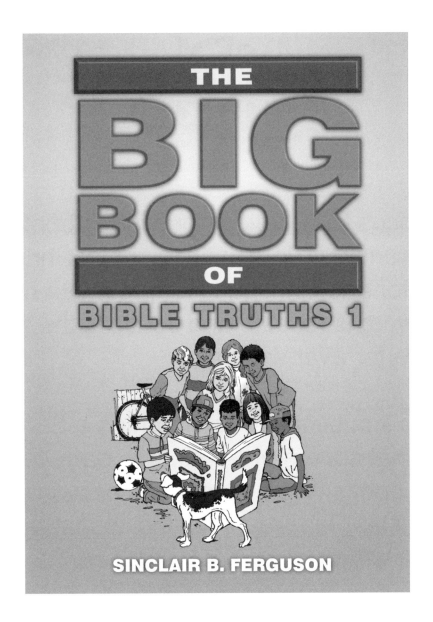

You can never have too many stories! Children love them: We all do! And who better to hear about in a story than the great storyteller himself, Jesus.

Through the stories in this book *The Big Book of Bible Truths 1* you will find out about Jesus, his life, how he wants to get to know you. Sinclair tells twenty-seven stories that will teach you about what it means to be a Christian.

Nicknames, moth burgers – there are many interesting stories that teach you things you didn't know before and loads of cool stuff about Jesus Christ, the Son of God. Illustrated throughout, this book is going to be another family favourite! Includes Extra Features: Bible reading; lesson summary; prayer.

ISBN: 978-1-84550-371-0

CHRISTIAN FOCUS PUBLICATIONS

Christian   Christian   CF4K   Mentor
Focus   Heritage

Christian Focus Publications publishes books for adults and children under its four main imprints: Christian Focus, CF4K, Mentor and Christian Heritage. Our books reflect that God's word is reliable and Jesus is the way to know him, and live for ever with him.

Our children's publication list includes a Sunday School curriculum that covers pre-school to early teens; puzzle and activity books. We also publish personal and family devotional titles, biographies and inspirational stories that children will love.

If you are looking for quality Bible teaching for children then we have an excellent range of Bible story and age specific theological books.

From pre-school to teenage fiction, we have it covered!

Find us at our web page:
www.christianfocus.com

CF4·K
Because you're never
too young to know Jesus